SPIRITUAL ABUSE
Breaking Free
from Religious Control

JUNE HUNT

ROSE PUBLISHING/ASPIRE PRESS

Torrance, California

ROSE PUBLISHING/ASPIRE PRESS

CONTENTS

Dear Friend,

Never will I forget her tears—the tears streaming down her cheeks. But not tears of sadness—rather tears of relief.

This young nurse—lovely, respectful, sincere—attended my home Bible study. As she listened intently, absorbing every morsel of truth, she finally blurted out, "All these years I've been living under the law—but not God's law! Now I'm being set free!"

Mona proceeded to explain, "I worked very hard in high school, and before graduation I received my class ring. But when I wore it to church, I was met with such condemnation, such negativity, such accusations." Because Mona desired to please the Lord, she never again put on the ring.

Another young woman, Laura, had given her heart to Christ as an adult. Her pastor pronounced, "Wearing jewelry is being a Jezebel." Laura deeply desired to please the Lord, so she wouldn't wear jewelry again. The pastor further proclaimed, "Wearing red is worldly." Laura deeply desired to please the Lord, so she wouldn't wear red again.

One day Laura came to church with a flower in her hair, but from the pulpit, the preacher rebuked her for looking like a harlot. In fact, all females who wore flowers in their hair—or on their clothing—were guilty ... guilty ... guilty. Wearing a flower was flaunting your sexuality. Laura deeply desired to please the Lord, so she wouldn't wear a flower again. Those condemning words hurt her heart—they crushed her spirit.

Personally, I had never heard that wearing red was wrong. "What else was prohibited?" I asked. She said, "Going to a fair or a musical—that's being in the world."

These and other similar restrictions raise questions we need to ask: What are man-made laws and what are God-given laws? Is a religious rule a righteous rule or merely a preacher's preference or a church's position? Is the religious rule based merely on private interpretation? Is it a cultural command or a correct command based on the whole counsel of God?

When I first taught on the topic of spiritual abuse, I wondered, *Does the Bible anywhere forbid wearing red?* When I did a word study (looking up every single reference to red, scarlet, and crimson, the answer was absolutely not! In fact, the most famous chapter in the Bible extolling the virtues of a righteous woman is Proverbs 31. And in this chapter, look at what this "Proverbs 31 Woman" does: She dresses her household in scarlet (v. 21)!

While any distortion or misapplication of God's Word is clearly wrong, God's judgment will fall greatest upon those who abuse their spiritual positions of trust for selfish gain, for sexual control, and for personal power. Ultimately control is the name of their game.

Truth originates with God as revealed through His Word. It does not originate with imperfect human beings who teach about the truth. Therefore, if you want to be wise about a certain issue, don't just follow a religious leader blindly, like a blind sheep. Don't just look at isolated Scriptures taken out of context but first look thoroughly at what God has already said. Ultimately, when you grasp the whole counsel of God on that subject, you will not fall prey to spiritual predators; neither will you be the victim of spiritual abuse.

Tragically, these victims are too trusting or too unknowing or they feel too powerless to do anything about the past or the present. However, those who have been victims of such abuse are not powerless. They simply need to learn how to appropriate the power of God and to live by His truth.

My prayer regarding this book on spiritual abuse is that through these pages those who are in bondage will find lasting freedom. Isn't it wonderful that Jesus exhorts you to know the truth because "the truth will set you free"!

Yours in the Lord's hope,

June Hunt

SPIRITUAL ABUSE
Breaking Free
from Religious Control

Think about it. Who in our society offends us the most? Isn't it the robbers, the killers, the rapists, the flagrant *law breakers*?

Now think about Jesus. Who in His society offended Him the most? Wasn't it the Pharisees, the religious leaders of the day, the legalistic *law keepers*? Didn't they upset Him the most?

But why the Pharisees? After all, they went to the temple, paid the tithes, read the Word, kept the Law, prayed the prayers. So why was Jesus offended most by the prominent law keepers?

The answer is clear. Although they were representatives of the house of God, they did not represent the heart of God. Christ called them *"hypocrites."* And He made it plain: They will be rewarded here on earth, but certainly not in heaven.

Jesus said ...

> "When you pray, do not be like the
> hypocrites, for they love to pray
> standing in the synagogues and on the
> street corners to be seen by others.
> Truly I tell you, they have
> received their reward in full."
> (Matthew 6:5)

DEFINITIONS

They can't believe their eyes when they see the disciples' hands. Dirty, unwashed hands, such a contrast to their own pristine palms.

These religious leaders strive to be the "picture" of perfection, so refined in their priestly garb. These prestigious Pharisees scrutinize the followers of Jesus who lift their food to their mouths with "unclean" hands—ceremonially defiled hands that have not been washed according to their customs.

▶ The Pharisees say: Beware—your unclean hands soil any hope of righteousness.

▶ Jesus says: No, what stains your righteousness is your *unclean hearts*.

> "What goes into someone's mouth
> does not defile them,
> but what comes out of their mouth,
> that is what defiles them."
> (Matthew 15:11)

The practice of spiritual abuse has persisted ever since the serpent in the Garden of Eden distorted and outright lied about God's words to Adam and Eve. In doing so, he managed to create doubt in their minds regarding the character of God and His relationship to those He had created. The result, of course, was that they found the thought of becoming like God more appealing than remaining dependent on God. That thought led them to trust Satan's words rather than God's words, and their descendants have struggled with this same problem ever since.[1]

The serpent said to Eve, *"Did God really say, 'You must not eat from any tree in the garden?'* ... *'You will not certainly die'* ... *'For God knows that when you eat from it your eyes will be opened, and you will be like God, knowing good and evil'"* (Genesis 3:1, 4–5). The serpent contradicted God's Word and seduced the first couple into taking the fatal bite!

Though the practice is age-old, the term "spiritual abuse" is relatively new. The following definitions explain how spiritual leaders can misuse their position of authority.

▶ **Spiritual abuse** is the mistreatment of a person by someone in a position of spiritual authority, resulting in diminishing that person's spiritual vitality and growth.[2]

▶ **Spiritual abuse** is the use of religious words or acts to manipulate someone for personal gain or to achieve a personal agenda, thereby harming that person's walk with God.

In his second letter to the Corinthians, Paul said, *"... we do not use deception, nor do we distort the word of God. On the contrary, by setting forth the truth plainly we commend ourselves to everyone's conscience in the sight of God"* (2 Corinthians 4:2).

▶ **Spiritual abuse** is putting confidence in your position of authority and your perceived right to use those under your influence to accomplish your own personal agenda. However, God alone has the right, the wisdom, and the power to accomplish His plans and purposes for those He has created.

"To the elders among you,
I appeal as a fellow elder and a witness of Christ's sufferings who also will share in the glory to be revealed:
Be shepherds of God's flock that is under your care, watching over them—not because you must, but because you are willing, as God wants you to be; not pursuing dishonest gain, but eager to serve; not lording it over those entrusted to you, but being examples to the flock."
(1 Peter 5:1–3)

QUESTION: "What is at the core of spiritual abuse?"

ANSWER: At the core of spiritual abuse is excessive control of others. Spiritual abuse is acting "spiritual" to benefit oneself by using self-centered efforts to control others.

A – **Acting spiritual to**

B – **Benefit oneself by**

U – **Using**

S – **Self-centered**

E – **Efforts to control others**

EXAMPLES

▶ The pastor who uses guilt or greed to compel attendance, financial giving, or service

▶ The spiritual leader who takes emotional or sexual advantage of a counselee in the name of "comfort or compassion"

▶ Religious people who accuse those who disagree with them of being rebellious against God

▶ The ministry head who demands absolute, unquestioned obedience no matter what, whether reasonable or not, whether biblical or not

> "Jesus said to them, 'The kings of the Gentiles lord it over them; and those who exercise authority over them call themselves Benefactors.'" (Luke 22:25)

Spiritual Abuse Is Not:

▶ **Administering church discipline**

- God commanded the church to administer church discipline for the purpose of correcting and restoring sinning Christians to fellowship with the Lord and with the church. Because the focus of church discipline is not on punishment, it must be administered prayerfully and in love. Church discipline is also intended to maintain the church's purity in belief and practice.

Example: The apostle Paul instructed the Corinthian church to discipline a sexually immoral man by removing him from their midst.

"Your boasting is not good. Don't you know that a little yeast [sin] *leavens the whole batch of dough* [church]? *Get rid of the old yeast, so that you may be a new unleavened batch—as you really are. For Christ, our Passover lamb, has been sacrificed"* (1 Corinthians 5:6–7).

▶ **Rejecting a person's incorrect theological beliefs**

- The church must evaluate those who teach the Bible to other church members. The church, as the "pillar and foundation of the truth," must reject incorrect interpretations and false teaching, just as Christ rejected the self-made righteousness and erroneous teachings of the Pharisees.

Example: The apostle Paul does not hesitate to identify those who would subvert the message of truth as being like those who opposed truth in the past.

"Just as Jannes and Jambres opposed Moses, so also these teachers oppose the truth. They are men of depraved minds, who, as far as the faith is concerned, are rejected" (2 Timothy 3:8).

WHAT IS Legalism?

Do this. Don't do that. Do this. Don't do that.

What was the purpose of the Old Testament Law, especially since we are not bound by it today? Simply stated, the hundreds upon hundreds of rules and regulations making up the Law reveal a supreme standard of holiness, a standard no human being can keep. The Law was never intended to leave God's people discouraged and in despair, but to first show them that they were sinners and then to lead them to a Savior who would not only pay the penalty for their sins and forgive their sins, but also give them power over sin and give them eternal life.

In other words, no one can keep the Law perfectly; therefore, no one can ever be saved by the Law! The requirement of the Law (perfection) shows us that we all need God's mercy and grace, which is found in Jesus alone. However, between the giving of the Law and the coming of Jesus, the religious leaders so distorted and mishandled the Law that it came to be viewed as the way to become righteous before God, making it a type of savior in and of itself.

According to this "distorted" law, the outward practice of "dos and don'ts" defined people as righteous, even though they woefully neglected the issues of the heart. Then, when the true Savior came, the religious leaders failed to recognize Him and condemned those who did. Therefore, Jesus adamantly opposed the religious legalism of His day and the spiritual abuse His people suffered at the hands of those whom God had entrusted with the Law generations earlier.

The apostle Paul said ...

> "Since they did not know
> the righteousness of God and sought to
> establish their own, they did not submit
> to God's righteousness. Christ is the
> culmination of the law so that there may be
> righteousness for everyone who believes."
> (Romans 10:3–4)

> "Clearly no one who relies on the law is
> justified before God, because
> 'the righteous will live by faith.'"
> (Galatians 3:11)

Whereas the general motive behind most spiritual abuse is power, the primary tool by which this power is gained is legalism.[3]

The following statements provide a comprehensive definition of legalism.

▶ **Legalism** is a system of living by the law in order to make spiritual progress and earn God's blessing.

▶ **Legalism** comes from the Latin word *legalis*, which means "law."[4]

▶ **Legalism** is a strict adherence to a code of "dos and don'ts" as a means of earning the approval of God.[5]

▶ **Legalism** is a misuse of the law, resulting in a *wrong* way of trying to appear *right*.

▶ **Legalism** is any attempt to gain or maintain God's favor by human effort.

Unfortunately, Israel was guilty of practicing legalism ...

" ... the people of Israel, who pursued the law as the way of righteousness, have not attained their goal. Why not? Because they pursued it not by faith but as if it were by works."
(Romans 9:31–32)

QUESTION: "What is at the core of legalism?"

ANSWER: At the core of legalism is a works mentality—looking to your own efforts to gain the acceptance of the Lord.

L – **Looking to your own**

E – **Efforts to**

G – **Gain the**

A – **Acceptance of the**

L – **Lord**

EXAMPLES

▶ The congregation that judges another congregation because of their manner of dress, style of worship, or the Bible translation they use

▶ The spiritual leader who looks down on some in the congregation, perceiving them to be spiritually immature and inferior

▶ The religious people who put confidence in "the flesh," which means living out of their own resources and their perceived achievement of a self-imposed standard of righteousness that causes them to despise others and to develop a prideful spirit

However, God alone knows the heart of a person. Only He can judge motives. The Bible says, *"All a person's ways seem pure to them, but motives are weighed by the LORD"* (Proverbs 16:2).

Legalism Is Not:

▶ **Establishing rules and regulations**

- Every organization, including churches, schools, businesses, and even homes, has rules and regulations. These are necessary for the organization to function properly.

Example: The apostle Paul instructed the Corinthian Church regarding how they should conduct their religious meetings.

"Two or three prophets should speak, and the others should weigh carefully what is said. And if a revelation comes to someone who is sitting down, the first speaker should stop. For you can all prophesy in turn so that everyone may be instructed and encouraged. The spirits of prophets are subject to the control of prophets. For God is not a God of disorder but of peace" (1 Corinthians 14:29–33).

▶ **Submitting to authority**

- God established authority figures in the church, home, and government for our good. These individuals are to meet the needs of those under their authority and provide them with leadership, guidance, protection, and accountability.

Example: The writer of the book of Hebrews explained the function of authority and how Christians are to relate to their leaders.

"Have confidence in your leaders and submit to their authority, because they keep watch over you as those who must give an account. Do this so that their work will be a joy, not a burden, for that would be of no benefit to you" (Hebrews 13:17).

▶ Having personal standards for Christian living

- Within the boundaries of biblical absolutes, God gives us the responsibility to choose how we will live our Christian lives. The choices we make throughout the day as to how we will present ourselves to others and how we will conduct ourselves around others reflect our standards. Making choices to live by biblical standards is not legalism, even if the choices are more conservative or restrictive than the choices of others.

Example: Through Joshua, God gave the Israelites the choice as to whether they would serve Him or not.

" ... choose for yourselves this day whom you will serve ... But as for me and my household, we will serve the LORD" (Joshua 24:15).

Power! It's invigorating, even intoxicating. And when unrestrained and unchecked, it can be characterized by the timeless adage—power corrupts.

In some ways they started out so right. The Pharisees esteemed the Law of Moses, rejected moves toward secularization, and swelled national pride through rightly honoring Jewish heritage.

But they ended up so wrong. Preoccupation with the Law turned into misapplication of the Law, rules took precedent over people, and nationalism spawned a sense of superiority toward others. This is the opposite picture of the requirements for the spiritual leaders in Christ's church.

"Since an overseer manages God's household, he must be blameless—not overbearing, not quick-tempered, not given to drunkenness, not violent, not pursuing dishonest gain.
Rather, he must be hospitable, one who loves what is good, who is self-controlled, upright, holy and disciplined."
(Titus 1:7–8)

Although many people have a heart for serving God and others, the following list includes positions in which spiritual abusers frequently commit their abuse.

▶ **Rigid, religious family members**

- Parents
- Husbands, wives
- Children
- Other relatives

▶ **Manipulative church members** (and equivalents in all religions)

- Pastors, priests, chaplains, bishops
- Missionaries, evangelists, prophets, apostles
- Bible teachers, mentors, disciplers, intercessors
- Choir members, choir directors, worship leaders

▶ **Covert occult practitioners**

- Fortune tellers, psychics, astrologers
- Spiritists, mediums
- Sorcerers, witches, witch doctors, shamans
- Necromancers

▶ **Mind-controlling cultists**

- Cult leaders
- Cult boards, council members

- Cult trainees
- Heretical sect members

▶ **Other deceivers and dominators**

- Manipulative televangelists, para-church ministry leaders
- Coercive counselors, therapists, advisers
- Religious bullies in neighborhoods, schools, workplaces
- Religious extremists, terrorists

Paul said to the Galatians ...

> "Some people are throwing you into confusion and are trying to pervert the gospel of Christ."
> (Galatians 1:7)

The Law given to the Israelites through Moses has been discussed and debated for centuries. While its meaning may appear quite clear and uncomplicated to the average person, the Hebrew religious leaders poured over it day and night, searching for secret and minute meanings to debate among themselves.

These students of the Law approached God's Law as a secular lawyer might approach civil law—as something for them to interpret and apply rather than something to simply obey. They considered it complicated and added "amendments" to it in order to "simplify" it for the common people. In so doing, they twisted and distorted it to the point that it was unrecognizable to its Author and became a stumbling block to salvation for those seeking to keep it.

Similarly, first-century Christians encountered contradictory opinions and criticism for teaching that Jesus had freed them from the demands of the Law. These contenders fell into basically three camps, and Christians today continue to face these same three errors of interpretation when trying to decide what to do with the Old Testament Law.[6]

▶ **Galatianism** is the commingling of law and grace, teaching that grace is given for salvation but the law is given for living (the false doctrine Paul corrected in the book of Galatians). It is performing good works in an attempt to attain perfection or holiness in order to keep what Christ has already made possible by His death and resurrection. This produces a stress-filled local church that sees God as a critical parent whose love and acceptance has to be earned. For this reason, Paul challenged the Church at Galatia ...

"Did you receive the Spirit by the works of the law, or by believing what you heard? Are you so foolish? After beginning by means of the Spirit, are you now trying to finish by means of the flesh?"
(Galatians 3:2–3)

▶ **Ceremonialism** is the teaching that certain ordinances, such as confession, baptism, and particular sacraments are essential to salvation and bring about God's favor. It is the commingling of rituals and grace, teaching that grace alone is not sufficient but must be accompanied by something else. This produces a pressure-filled local church that seeks to do enough good deeds to both gain and retain God's approval. The church at Antioch was exposed to such teaching ...

"Certain people came down from Judea to Antioch and were teaching the believers: 'Unless you are circumcised, according to the custom taught by Moses, you cannot be saved.'"
(Acts 15:1)

▶ **Antinomianism** is the teaching that under the gospel of grace, a person is free from any moral law or standard. Faith alone is necessary for salvation; therefore, all rules for living are soundly rejected. It comes from the Greek words *anti*, which means "against," and *nomos*, which means "law," that is, "against the law."[7] This produces a confusion-filled local church that mistakes liberty in Christ for license to sin, keeping its members in slavery to sinful, fleshly desires and in conflict with God's Word. The early Christian church was challenged by this false concept ...

"Certain individuals whose condemnation was written about long ago have secretly slipped in among you.
They are ungodly people, who pervert the grace of our God into a license for immorality and deny Jesus Christ our only Sovereign and Lord."
(Jude 4)

QUESTION: "Is there no law for Christians to live by?"[8]

ANSWER: The Bible says that under the New Covenant, God will put His law in the minds and the hearts of every Christian. Additionally, whether or not they know the Law of Moses or receive the Holy Spirit, all people receive the gift of conscience from God to distinguish between right and wrong.

According to Romans 2:14–15, *"When Gentiles, who do not have the law, do by nature things required by the law, they are a law for themselves, even though they do not have the law. They show that the requirements of the law are written on their hearts, their consciences also bearing witness, and their thoughts sometimes accusing them and at other times even defending them."*

Since the Spirit of Christ indwells every true Christian, we possess new desires and new capabilities to do His will.

> "This is the covenant I will make with them after that time, says the Lord.
> I will put my laws in their hearts, and I will write them on their minds."
> (Hebrews 10:16)

▶ **He prompts** you to desire and to do His will.

" ... *for it is God who works in you to will and to act in order to fulfill his good purpose"* (Philippians 2:13).

▶ **He provides** you with the power to do what He calls you to do.

"The one who calls you is faithful, and he will do it" (1 Thessalonians 5:24).

They are at it again, trying to trip up the Teacher. The religious leaders of the day reject the teaching and ministry of Jesus and are doggedly determined to disgrace Him publicly with complicated, manipulative questions. He silences them each and every time with perfect wisdom, but they persist.

During the quiet of dawn in the temple courts, Jesus sits down to teach, but commotion breaks out. The Pharisees drag a woman to stand before Jesus in utter humiliation, claiming she was caught in the very act of adultery. It is an opportune moment, the Pharisees connive to "catch" Jesus once and for all and curtail His ministry. They will do anything and use anyone to satiate their sinful quest. And so they ask Him, *"Teacher, this woman was caught in the act of adultery. In the Law Moses commanded us to stone such women. Now what do you say?"* (John 8:4–5).

The difference between law and grace is about to be displayed. While the Pharisees keep firing away with questions, Jesus is silent and writes on the ground with His finger. Then He stands up and replies: *"Let any one of you who is without sin be the first to throw a stone at her"* (John 8:7). Wisdom speaks and silences once again. One by one the people leave the temple courts. Jesus and the accused woman are alone, and grace again is dispensed. Jesus tells her that He does not condemn her, but exhorts her to repent and pursue righteousness. He says, *"Go now and leave your life of sin"* (John 8:11).

Law vs. Grace

DEALS WITH

LAW: External Regulations

> *"Since you died with Christ to the elemental spiritual forces of this world, why, as though you still belonged to the world, do you submit to its rules: 'Do not handle! Do not taste! Do not touch!'?"* (Colossians 2:20–21).

GRACE: Inner Heart Attitude

> *"For in my inner being I delight in God's law ... "* (Romans 7:22).

RELATES DOING/BEING

LAW: "Do in order to be."

> *"Is the law, therefore, opposed to the promises of God? Absolutely not! For if a law had been given that could impart life, then righteousness would certainly have come by the law"* (Galatians 3:21).

GRACE: "You are, therefore, do."

> *"For you were once darkness, but now you are light in the Lord. Live as children of light ... "* (Ephesians 5:8).

OPERATING PRINCIPLE

LAW: Try harder through work and effort.

"For all who rely on the works of the law are under a curse, as it is written: 'Cursed is everyone who does not continue to do everything written in the Book of the Law'" (Galatians 3:10).

GRACE: Receive, trust, rest.

"Come to me, all you who are weary and burdened, and I will give you rest" (Matthew 11:28).

TYPE OF SYSTEM

LAW: Achieving System

"But the people of Israel, who pursued the law as the way of righteousness, have not attained their goal. Why not? Because they pursued it not by faith but as if it were by works. They stumbled over the stumbling stone" (Romans 9:31–32).

GRACE: Receiving System

"For it is by grace you have been saved, through faith—and this is not from yourselves, it is the gift of God—not by works, so that no one can boast" (Ephesians 2:8–9).

FOCUS

LAW: Bondage/Obligation

"It is for freedom that Christ has set us free. Stand firm, then, and do not let yourselves be burdened again by a yoke of slavery. ... Again I declare to every man who lets himself be circumcised that he is obligated to obey the whole law" (Galatians 5:1, 3).

GRACE: Release/Freedom

"But now, by dying to what once bound us, we have been released from the law so that we serve in the new way of the Spirit, and not in the old way of the written code" (Romans 7:6).

RESULTS

LAW: Fear/Rejection/Condemnation

"For whoever keeps the whole law and yet stumbles at just one point is guilty of breaking all of it" (James 2:10).

GRACE: Forgiveness/Acceptance/Reconciliation

"For I will forgive their wickedness and will remember their sins no more" (Hebrews 8:12).

LIVES OUT OF

LAW: Flesh—man's resources

"Are you so foolish? After beginning by means of the Spirit, are you now trying to finish by means of the flesh?" (Galatians 3:3).

GRACE: Spirit—God's resources

" ... because through Christ Jesus the law of the Spirit who gives life has set you free from the law of sin and death" (Romans 8:2).

PURPOSE

LAW: To show us our sin and our need to be right with God

"Therefore no one will be declared righteous in God's sight by the works of the law; rather, through the law we become conscious of our sin" (Romans 3:20).

GRACE: To make us right with God

"But now apart from the law the righteousness of God has been made known, to which the Law and the Prophets testify. This righteousness is given through faith in Jesus Christ to all who believe. There is no difference between Jew and Gentile" (Romans 3:21–22).

TERMS

LAW: Our responsibility

"The LORD your God commands you this day to follow these decrees and laws; carefully observe them with all your heart and with all your soul" (Deuteronomy 26:16).

GRACE: Our gift from God

"For the wages of sin is death, but the gift of God is eternal life in Christ Jesus our Lord" (Romans 6:23).

MOTIVATION

LAW: Fear/Reward

"'Cursed is anyone who does not uphold the words of this law by carrying them out.' Then all the people shall say, 'Amen!' If you fully obey the LORD your God and carefully follow all his commands I give you today, the LORD your God will set you

high above all the nations on earth. All these blessings will come on you and accompany you if you obey the LORD your God" (Deuteronomy 27:26—28:1–2).

GRACE: Love

"*For Christ's love compels us, because we are convinced that one died for all, and therefore all died*" (2 Corinthians 5:14).

WHAT QUESTIONS concerning the Law Cause Confusion?

They are spiritual leaders devoid of the Spirit. They say they esteem the Law of Moses, but desecrate it daily by their pride and hypocrisy. The Pharisees, Israel's supposed spiritual shepherds, frustrate their flock with additional man-made traditions they themselves don't keep.

Jesus is trying to teach a new way—to please God in the power of the Spirit, to engage the heart, mind, and will in obeying God's commands. But the Pharisees will have nothing of it. Their rejection—their rebellion—against the very God they claim to serve reaps harsh rebuke from Jesus Himself.

"Woe to you, teachers of the law and Pharisees, you hypocrites! You clean the outside of the cup and dish, but inside they are full of greed and self-indulgence. ... Woe to you, blind guides!"
(Matthew 23:25, 16)

QUESTION: "Is the law wrong?"

ANSWER: No. The Law is the revelation of God's perfect standard of righteousness. The Bible says ...

> "The law is holy, and the commandment is holy, righteous and good."
> (Romans 7:12)

QUESTION: "According to Scripture, was the law abolished?"

ANSWER: No, Jesus didn't abolish the law. He fulfilled it. That means the standard still exists, but the methodology for attaining that standard has changed from self-effort to Spirit-empowerment from works to grace.

> "Do not think that I have come to abolish the Law or the Prophets; I have not come to abolish them but to fulfill them."
> (Matthew 5:17)

QUESTION: "What does 'Jesus fulfilled it' mean?"

ANSWER: The Law was a covenant, an agreement, a contract. Just as a builder is under a contract to build a house, once the house is complete, the contract is fulfilled. The builder does not continue to work at building the house any longer. Likewise, Jesus fulfilled the requirements of the contract (the Law) through His teaching and actions. He accomplished what we could never do by our own efforts. Then the Law-Keeper became the sacrifice for us, the lawbreakers. The Bible says ...

"Christ is the culmination of the law so that there may be righteousness for everyone who believes." (Romans 10:4)

QUESTION: "What is the difference between legalism and biblical obedience?"

ANSWER: Legalism is conforming outwardly to God's or man's standard for righteous behavior while ignoring God's standard for righteous attitudes, convictions, values, and thoughts. Biblical obedience is conforming outwardly to God's righteous standard while being conformed inwardly to the character of Christ through the enabling grace of God.

▶ In **legalism**, the resource is *self-effort*—the motive is self-promotion. Legalism results in pride and approaching God on the basis of your performance.

▶ In **obedience**, the resource is the *Spirit of God*— the motive is to glorify God. Obedience results in humility and approaching God on the basis of Christ's performance.

In Christ Jesus God has fulfilled His promise.

"I will give you a new heart and put a new spirit in you; I will remove from you your heart of stone and give you a heart of flesh. And I will put my Spirit in you and move you to follow my decrees and be careful to keep my laws." (Ezekiel 36:26–27)

CHARACTERISTICS

They come from opposite sides of the tracks. One is refined, respected, and revered—after all, he is a Pharisee. He has an "in" with God. The other is despised, disdained, and dejected—after all, he's a tax collector. He is a spiritual "outcast." While both say something to God, the tax collector can't look up, but the Pharisee stands up: *"God, I thank you that I am not like other people—robbers, evildoers, adulterers—or even like this tax collector. I fast twice a week and give a tenth of all I get"* (Luke 18:11–12).

So goes the prayer of the Pharisee. Standing aside, the tax collector beats his chest and pours out his heart: *"God, have mercy on me, a sinner"* (v. 13).

Jesus speaks this parable to those who trust in their own righteousness, who exercise spiritual snobbery toward any who don't "measure up." The tax collector expresses a humble dependency on God resulting in the forgiveness of his sins. Jesus says ...

> "I tell you that this man, rather than the other, went home justified before God. For all those who exalt themselves will be humbled, and those who humble themselves will be exalted."
> (Luke 18:14)

While some religious groups are free of abuse, others are occasionally abusive, and still others are intensely abusive. The people especially vulnerable to systemic spiritual abuse belong to groups where all the power is at the top and average members are subject to the dictates of those over them. Therefore, the structure of a religious organization is of paramount importance in identifying the probability of spiritual abuse.

The apostle Peter reflected the heart of humility vital for every spiritual leader when he said ...

"To the elders among you,
I appeal as a fellow elder and a witness of Christ's sufferings who also will share in the glory to be revealed:
Be shepherds of God's flock that is under your care, watching over them—
not because you must, but because you are willing, as God wants you to be;
not pursuing dishonest gain, but eager to serve; not lording it over those entrusted to you, but being examples to the flock."
(1 Peter 5:1–3)

Spiritually Abusive Leaders Are ...

▶ **Authoritarian**[9]

- Implying that God communicates with His people only through a hierarchy of power

- Claiming to have been called and established by God Himself

- Boasting that the leaders speak for God and expecting followers to support and obey them without question

But the Bible says, *"Those who exalt themselves will be humbled, and those who humble themselves will be exalted"* (Matthew 23:12).

▶ **Image-Conscious**[10]

- Seeking to present an image of perfect righteousness

- Misrepresenting their personal history to wrongly portray a special relationship to God

- Minimizing or covering up their mistakes and character flaws

- Covering up physical and sexual abuse within the church

But the Bible says, *"Woe to you, teachers of the law and Pharisees, you hypocrites! You are like whitewashed tombs, which look beautiful on the outside but on the inside are full of the bones of the dead and everything unclean"* (Matthew 23:27).

▶ Suppressive of Criticism

- Determining all issues at the top level of the organization and demanding compliance by the members

- Curtailing individual thinking by saying that such individuality leads to division and doubts about God

- Maintaining that those who question or seek to correct anything about the organization are actually challenging God's authority

But the Bible says, *"A rebuke impresses a discerning person more than a hundred lashes a fool. ... Whoever loves discipline loves knowledge, but whoever hates correction is stupid"* (Proverbs 17:10; 12:1).

▶ Perfectionistic[11]

- Demanding flawless obedience

- Condemning failure of any type or magnitude

- Promoting pride, elitism, and arrogance

But the Bible says, *"Pride goes before destruction, a haughty spirit before a fall"* (Proverbs 16:18).

▶ Unbalanced

- Flaunting their distinctiveness to validate their claim of having a "special" relationship with God

- Carrying biblical law to the extreme

- Majoring on the minor issues

But the Bible says, *"Woe to you Pharisees, because you give God a tenth of your mint, rue and all other kinds of garden herbs, but you neglect justice and the love of God. You should have practiced the latter without leaving the former undone"* (Luke 11:42).

▶ Coercive[12]

- Using any tactic available to convince followers to disregard their own logic and do what the leaders demand

- Demanding submission by claiming that the messages they receive come directly from God

- Deluding members by presenting themselves as the only ones who can properly interpret God's Word to the people

But the Bible says, *"They want to be teachers of the law, but they do not know what they are talking about or what they so confidently affirm"* (1 Timothy 1:7).

▶ Intimidating[13]

- Threatening members routinely with punishment or excommunication in order to gain compliance

- Holding the possibility of eternal condemnation over the heads of followers in order to force submission

- Predicting financial ruin or physical calamity for disobedient members in order to assure obedience

But the Bible says, *"Woe to you shepherds ... who only take care of yourselves! Should not shepherds take care of the flock? You eat the curds, clothe yourselves with the wool and slaughter the choice animals, but you do not take care of the flock"* (Ezekiel 34:2–3).

▶ Terrorizing[14]

- Imparting fear, shame, self-doubt, identity confusion, and guilt to members

- Blaming problems within the organization on the sinfulness of the congregation

- Overemphasizing the problems of followers and presenting strict obedience as the only solution

But the Bible says, *"You have not strengthened the weak or healed the sick or bound up the injured. You have not brought back the strays or searched for the lost. You have ruled them harshly and brutally"* (Ezekiel 34:4).

▶ Condemning[15]

- Heaping condemnation on outsiders and anyone who leaves the congregation

- Teaching that followers will join the ranks of the condemned if they deviate from the teachings of the leaders

- Scapegoating individual members for failures within the organization

But the Bible says, *"How can you say to your brother, 'Let me take the speck out of your eye,' when all the time there is a plank in your own eye?"* (Matthew 7:4).

▶ Discriminating[16]

- Promoting church hierarchy

- Responding to people according to their titles and roles

- Instructing average members that their needs are less important than the needs of the leaders

But the Bible says, *"Beware of the teachers of the law. They like to walk around in flowing robes and love to be greeted with respect in the marketplaces and have the most important seats in the synagogues and the places of honor at banquets"* (Luke 20:46).

▶ Legalistic[17]

- Communicating that approval and acceptance are based on performance and position within the organization

- Burdening the people with excessive demands supposedly given by God directly to the leaders

- Expecting members to make extreme sacrifices of money, time, and energy for the sake of the organization

But the Bible says, *"Woe to those who make unjust laws, to those who issue oppressive decrees ... "* (Isaiah 10:1).

▶ Isolating[18]

- Defining relationships outside the congregation as negative and destructive

- Presenting the outside world as a place of egregious sin and temptation without any redeeming qualities

- Encouraging members to minimize or discontinue contact with family, friends, and the outside world

But the Bible says, *"Anyone who does not provide for their relatives, and especially for their own household, has denied the faith and is worse than an unbeliever"* (1 Timothy 5:8).

Legalism is basically an attitude in which God is seen as quick-to-judge—a stern taskmaster and a judgmental judge and arbiter of punishment. The attitude toward oneself is a misplaced confidence that leads to frustration, failure, and self-condemnation. The attitude toward others is prideful exclusivity that produces frustration, fear, and resentment in others.

In Philippians 3:6, the apostle Paul spoke of his own former *"righteousness based on the law"* as *"faultless"* in persecuting the early church and causing fear in believers.

> "Saul began to destroy the church.
> Going from house to house,
> he dragged off both men and women and
> put them in prison."
> (Acts 8:3)

As with all types of abuse, certain circumstances are more conducive than others for a spiritual "wolf" to take advantage of an unsuspecting "sheep." If you suspect spiritual abuse might be occurring, check to see whether a number of the traits summarized below apply to the spiritual leader.

▶ **Authoritarian**: demanding unquestioned obedience

▶ **Controlling**: invading aspects of life better left to the individual

▶ **Performance driven**: emphasizing external rather than internal qualities

▶ **Hypocritical**: employing a veneer of spirituality to cover carnal motives

▶ **Rigid**: devising elaborate, extra-biblical guidelines for members to follow

▶ **Deceitful**: twisting the truth of the Word to fit their own opinions and desires

Remember these words from Proverbs, the book of wisdom ...

"The simple believe anything,
but the prudent give thought to their steps."
(Proverbs 14:15)

Separating from a spiritually abusive group can be grueling because the leaders use fear, false guilt, and shame to keep members from leaving. Regardless of the difficulty, if you are in such a group, the Bible says you must leave—your spiritual life depends on it!

"If anyone teaches otherwise and does not consent to wholesome words, even the words of our Lord Jesus Christ, and to the doctrine which accords with godliness, he is proud, knowing nothing, but is obsessed with disputes and arguments over words, from which come envy, strife, reviling, evil suspicions ... From such withdraw yourself" (1 Timothy 6:3–5 NKJV).

For every abuse that your church has committed, repeat the following out loud:

"It was inappropriate for my church to (_name abuse_). I renounce this practice/position and announce my allegiance to God and to His Word."

Pray the following prayer of King David every day to reaffirm your reliance on God to guard and protect you.

"Since you are my rock and my fortress, for the sake of your name lead and guide me. Keep me free me from the trap that is set for me, for you are my refuge."
(Psalm 31:3–4)

Spiritually Abusive Groups Checklist

Ask yourself the following questions to determine whether a group is abusive and/or spiritually deceptive.

- ☐ Do they exalt someone as an *irrefutable authority* in the group?

- ☐ Do they discourage my *questions*?

- ☐ Do they demand my *absolute allegiance*?

- ☐ Do they have a long list of *rules* related to dress, hairstyle, or activities?

- ☐ Do they *judge* those who do not keep their list of rules?

- ☐ Do they consider themselves the *"only true church"*?

- ☐ Do they insist on making my major *life decisions* for me?

- ☐ Do they consider *those who leave* their group "apostates," "backsliders," or "doomed"?

- ☐ Do they *shame* people publicly?

Diseases have accompanying symptoms such as fever and specific aches and pains. The symptoms are not the problem, but rather are the result of the real problem, which is the disease itself. Likewise, legalism produces symptoms that some people mistake for the real problem.

Ultimately, legalistic abusers cause their victims to be overly burdened with responsibilities and kept so busy that they have difficulty processing any liberating truth. They become stricken with a disabling apathy toward gaining a deeper knowledge, intellectually put to sleep by constantly being told what to believe. Since they cannot adequately think for themselves, they become depersonalized and unable to function as God intended. For these reasons, Jesus sternly addressed the legalistic abusers of His day ...

"Jesus replied, 'And you experts in the law, woe to you, because you load people down with burdens they can hardly carry, and you yourselves will not lift one finger to help them. ...
Woe to you experts in the law, because you have taken away the key to knowledge. You yourselves have not entered, and you have hindered those who were entering.'"
(Luke 11:46, 52)

Spiritual Abuse Checklist

As you read the following symptoms, check to see whether you are a victim of a legalistic abuser:[19]

Low Self-Worth

☐ Do you think you must accept abuse?

☐ Do you think you must accept blame?

☐ Do you think you must accept condemnation?

Inordinate Fear

☐ Do you fear disapproval or condemnation?

☐ Do you fear authority figures?

☐ Do you fear conflict?

Excessive Guilt

☐ Do you feel like a failure?

☐ Do you feel a sense of shame?

☐ Do you feel a heaviness of heart?

Unresolved Anger

☐ Do you feel frustrated for not being perfect?

☐ Do you feel angry for not keeping all the rules?

☐ Do you feel that you are losing patience with yourself and others?

Limited Transparency

☐ Do you think you must put up a false front to hide the real you?

☐ Do you think if others really knew you, they would reject you?

☐ Do you think closeness with others is to be avoided?

Troubled Relationships

☐ Do you have difficulty saying *no*?

☐ Do you feel you are not forgiven?

☐ Do you continually compare yourself with others, keeping them at a distance?

High Self-Sufficiency

☐ Do you try to earn love by performing well?

☐ Do you try to do everything perfectly so as not to be rejected?

☐ Do you try to be in control in order to feel a sense of significance?

Misplaced Priorities

☐ Do you prioritize the externals, such as complying with rules and regulations?

☐ Do you have difficulty setting boundaries?

☐ Do you place importance on outward actions rather than on inward needs?

CAUSES

What are the beliefs behind legalism?

Trying to maintain God's acceptance is a full-time job for legalists. Thinking of God as a judge is more realistic an image in the minds of legalists than the image of God as a father who grants blessings to His children. But God's Word tells us that we are accepted by God through our acceptance of Christ, not through our human efforts. Christians will not experience God's judgment, for Christ experienced judgment *for them* at Calvary.

The Bible says ...

> " ... Christ was sacrificed once
> to take away the sins of many;
> and he will appear a second time,
> not to bear sin, but to bring salvation to
> those who are waiting for him."
> (Hebrews 9:28)

For many reasons people are susceptible to and then become snared by those who are legalistic or spiritually abusive. Some of those reasons include the following.

HAVING LEGALISTIC PARENTS ...

▶ Legalism in the home either trains children to perform well in order to please or drives children to rebel against the rigidity and hypocrisy found in legalists.

▶ Children with legalistic authority figures tend to view God as harsh, demanding, unmerciful, and unforgiving—a perception that breeds fear-driven compliance.

... PRESENTS REAL PROBLEMS

▶ Legalism does not create a climate of love for God based on His love for us nor does it encourage a heart inclined to please Him by living according to His Word.

▶ Children thrive on being raised in a Christian home by loving, godly parents—parents who accurately reflect God as a compassionate Father, who comforts us in our difficulties, disciplines us in love, and mercifully meets our needs.

The Bible says, *"Praise be to the God and Father of our Lord Jesus Christ, the Father of compassion and the God of all comfort, who comforts us in all our troubles"* (2 Corinthians 1:3–4).

"Every good and perfect gift is from above, coming down from the Father of the heavenly lights, who does not change like shifting shadows" (James 1:17).

FEELING INSIGNIFICANT AND UNACCEPTABLE TO GOD ...

▶ Legalism provides an "exact ruler" based on the extremely high standards of the legalistic leaders—an objective way to measure where you stand with God and where you fail to measure up.

▶ Legalism provides discipline—perfectionistic people become model disciples in a legalistic environment where acceptance is based solely on performance.

... PRESENTS REAL PROBLEMS

▶ Legalism tends to increase guilt rather than relieve it. Further, it fails to provide assurance of salvation.

▶ Rather than demonstrating humility before God, legalists become either prideful or so discouraged they give up on God altogether.

The Bible says, *"God opposes the proud but shows favor to the humble"* (1 Peter 5:5).

BEING PRESSURED BY OTHERS ...

▶ Legalists feel entitled. They present themselves as having spiritual authority and, therefore, as being entitled to receive immediate agreement and unquestioned compliance.

▶ Legalistic peers condemn those who disagree and accept those who agree with them, creating immense pressure for conformity.

... PRESENTS REAL PROBLEMS

- Legalism cannot make all people think, feel, reason, or believe the same way nor can it provide God's "rest," which comes from knowing that He loves and accepts us all just as we are.

- Christians need to share their spiritual struggles with one another so that they can pray for one another and grow in God's grace together. Doing so can create deep bonds of Christian love and intimate relationships.

The Bible says, *"Confess your sins to each other and pray for each other so that you may be healed. The prayer of a righteous person is powerful and effective"* (James 5:16).

BELONGING TO A LEGALISTIC CHURCH THAT LACKS GRACE ...

▶ Legalism emphasizes "doing"—witnessing, discipling, teaching, attending all required activities, and whatever else is expected.

▶ Legalistic activity flows out of a need to perform for God in order to meet His requirements for righteousness and to gain His approval.

▶ Legalism cannot give people the spiritual security that comes only in being assured of God's forgiveness and unconditional love and acceptance.

▶ Christian activity flows out of love for God and the grace of God.

The Bible says, *"God is able to bless you abundantly, so that in all things at all times, having all that you need, you will abound in every good work"* (2 Corinthians 9:8).

WHY ARE the Abused Drawn to Spiritual Abusers?

Victims of spiritual abuse typically feel that they need to work in order to please God or that they need to be punished by God for displeasing Him. The guilt they feel can be based on *true* guilt for their actual, unconfessed sin. More often, however, they have *false* guilt for actual sin that has already been forgiven or *false* guilt for imagined sin. This type of person usually has had a series of abusive relationships, often beginning with excessively rigid parents or authority figures.

The people following Jesus had been brought up believing their righteous works would save them.

"Then they asked him, 'What must we do to do the works God requires?' Jesus answered, 'The work of God is this: to believe in the one he has sent'" (John 6:28–29).

▶ **Grew up being abused or manipulated by someone they loved**

- Unjustly and severely disciplined for minor or imagined infractions

- Coerced into complying with wishes of parents

▶ **Were neglected by or inappropriately controlled by one or both parents**

- Ignored or made to feel insignificant

- Held responsible for meeting the emotional needs of parents

▶ **Have been systematically shamed or put down**

- Humiliated in front of others or made to feel like a bad person

- Called degrading names or constantly criticized

▶ **Come from demanding homes**

- Unable to please parents

- Expected to always excel and to never make mistakes

▶ **View God as a tyrant who imposes impossible standards**

- Perceive God to be a "watch dog" waiting to punish every bad thought or action, no matter how small or insignificant

- Feel that God has unrealistic expectations and that He is impossible to please

▶ **Obsess about blame and guilt**

- Constantly focus on personal faults and failures

- Live with persistent feelings of self-reproach and regret

▶ **Cannot accept grace and forgiveness**

- Persuaded that personal accountability and payment for sin cannot be transferred to another

- Driven by a strong need to suffer personally and pay for wrongdoings

▶ **Have low self-worth**

- Convinced that they have little or no value

- Feel inferior to others and undeserving

Those enslaved to a mind-set that keeps them captive in a cycle of abuse need to heed the words of the apostle Paul: *"See to it that no one takes you captive through hollow and deceptive philosophy, which depends on human tradition and the elemental spiritual forces of this world rather than on Christ"* (Colossians 2:8).

If you have found yourself in a spiritually abusive relationship, you can be sure that certain situations made you susceptible to it and kept you in it. Discovering what those situations are will be helpful as you seek to walk in freedom.

In order to identify the thinking patterns that led you into the abusive relationship, evaluate your wrong thinking—then you can change your thoughts, which will change your choices, which will change your actions, which will change your life![20]

Like Job, what you think about will determine how you feel and ultimately will direct your decision making ...

> "When I think about this, I am terrified; trembling seizes my body."
> (Job 21:6)

The apostle Paul gave this warning ...

> " ... watch out for those who cause divisions and put obstacles in your way that are contrary to the teaching you have learned. Keep away from them."
> (Romans 16:17)

Wrong Thinking Checklist

Ask yourself ...

☐ Do I think I should not hold spiritual authorities accountable for their actions?

☐ Do I think it is wrong for me to ask questions in church?

☐ Do I think I am too sinful or unspiritual to read the Bible for myself?

☐ Do I think I must obey a list of unwritten rules?

☐ Do I think it is okay for me to be judgmental?

☐ Do I think God wants me to have excessive guilt?

☐ Do I think I should be shamed because of my sin?

☐ Do I think I cannot or should not make decisions for myself?

☐ Do I think I deserve to feel guilty for leaving the church?

☐ Do I think I should go back to the abusive church?

☐ Do I think I am too sinful for God to ever forgive me?

☐ Do I think I am unworthy of God's love even though Jesus died for me?

QUESTION: "Why does God allow spiritual abuse?"

Answer: This question—phrased in different ways—is asked in every country and every culture: "How can a loving, all-powerful God permit abuse?" But even further, why would He permit *spiritual abuse*? Just as the question is logical, so is the answer.

▶ When God created Adam and Eve, He gave them "free will." This means they were not programmed like robots to do His will. They were given "choice." Their freedom allowed them the possibility of going against God's will—even to the extent of abusing someone else.

▶ Being "free" means not only having the opportunity to choose wrong but also the ability to do wrong. This is exactly what the original couple did: They chose to exercise their free will by doing what was against God's will. Thus, sin entered the human race.

▶ God made spiritual abuse possible only by giving human beings free will, but human beings make spiritual abuse actual by choosing to sin. Ultimately, God allows sin, but human beings cause sin by the choices they make.

As the Bible says ...

"This is the verdict: Light has come into the world, but people loved darkness instead of light because their deeds were evil."
(John 3:19)

Although God allows spiritual abuse, He hates it! Those who are godly will hate it also. Proverbs 8:13 says, *"To fear the LORD is to hate evil; I hate pride and arrogance, evil behavior and perverse speech."*

Know that He will execute His justice toward those who sin against Him and who spiritually wound His followers. The Bible clearly states ...

> "Do not take revenge, my dear friends,
> but leave room for God's wrath,
> for it is written: 'It is mine to avenge;
> I will repay,' says the Lord."
> (Romans 12:19)

WHAT IS the Root Cause of Spiritual Abuse?

Isn't it interesting how shifting the blame to God—or someone else—is much easier than taking personal responsibility for our wrong choices? Everyone is born with three inner needs—the needs for love, significance, and security.[21] Attempting to meet these three inner needs illegitimately creates within abusers a false sense of significance and within victims who accept abuse a false sense of security. Those inner needs seem to be met, at least for the moment. But those feelings don't last.

The Bible says ...

> "My God will meet all your needs according
> to the riches of his glory in Christ Jesus."
> (Philippians 4:19)

► WRONG BELIEF OF THE ABUSER

"God has given me special authority that sets me above others and entitles me to special treatment. I have more authority, and I know God's will better than others. Therefore, I deserve to have obedience from others. My way is God's way—I should not be questioned. My will is His will—I should not be denied."

A frequently quoted verse spoken by spiritual abusers is, *"Do not touch my anointed ones; do my prophets no harm"* (Psalm 105:15).

RIGHT BELIEF

"As the Lord's appointed 'under-shepherd,' I am to protect and provide for the flock of God with a heart totally committed to Him and His Holy Word. I am to love God and serve His people with my whole heart, and I am to live a life worthy of His calling. As God's shepherd, I am to lay down my life for His sheep just as He laid down His life for me and for them."

The Beloved Apostle John stated this clearly and succinctly, *"This is how we know what love is: Jesus Christ laid down his life for us. And we ought to lay down our lives for our brothers and sisters"* (1 John 3:16).

► WRONG BELIEF OF THE ABUSED

"God's acceptance of me is dependent on my keeping His laws as revealed by His special messengers. That is the only way I can earn His approval."

The devoted apostle Paul addressed this faulty belief clearly and definitively ...

"Are you so foolish? After beginning by means of the Spirit, are you now trying to finish by means of the flesh?" (Galatians 3:3).

RIGHT BELIEF

"God's Law shows me my sins and leads me to Christ, who alone can save me from sin. Because my faith is in Christ, not in the law, I am free in Christ. The Spirit of Christ, who lives in me, gives me the desire and the power to overcome sin in my life and to live in a way that pleases Him."

As the Bible says, *"The law was our guardian until Christ came that we might be justified by faith. Now that faith has come, we are no longer under a guardian"* (Galatians 3:24–25).

QUESTION: "How can being spiritually abused damage your relationship with God?"

ANSWER: When children hear the name "God," they subconsciously think about their own fathers—or the most authoritative figure in their lives—and then superimpose the characteristics of that adult onto God.

If the person in authority is trustworthy, the child considers God trustworthy. If the adult is untrustworthy, the child considers God untrustworthy.

As a result, the child's ability to trust in a loving God is severely damaged. Thus, when "spiritual shepherds" misuse the privilege of their position, many of the flock lose faith—feeling they cannot entrust their lives to the Lord for salvation. In their minds, those who represent themselves as being God's special messengers are a reflection of God Himself. If they are abusive and untrustworthy, then God is also abusive and untrustworthy. However, such logic is grossly flawed and leads many abuse victims astray. That is why every victim of abuse needs to take to heart these words of encouragement ...

"Trust in the LORD with all your heart and
lean not on your own understanding;
in all your ways submit to him, and he will
make your paths straight."
(Proverbs 3:5–6)

HOW CAN You Be Set Free?

It's nighttime. Why *wouldn't* he come during the night hour under the cover of darkness? Why *wouldn't* he fear upsetting his fellow religious Pharisees? In truth, he's not like most of the Pharisees: prideful, pompous, and puffed-up. This humble seeker of truth truly respects Jesus as a teacher. But now, what he hears doesn't make sense. Nicodemus—a Pharisee, a member of the Sanhedrin—tries to make sense of the shocking statement made by Jesus: *"Very truly I tell you, no one can see the kingdom of God unless they are born again"* (John 3:3).

Born again? Nicodemus asks, *"How can someone be born when they are old? ... Surely they cannot enter a second time into their mother's womb to be born!"* (John 3:4).

Patiently, Jesus explains that this birth far exceeds any physical birth. Then He emphatically states, *"You must be born again"* (John 3:7)—literally meaning "born from above."

Jesus leaves Nicodemus no option. Likewise, He leaves us no option. It's not enough to be physically alive. We also need to be spiritually alive. If we want to hear the counsel of God, we can't be spiritually dead. We must be spiritually alive. We must be born again! We must be born of the Spirit!

How the Savior Sets You Free

FOUR POINTS OF GOD'S PLAN

#1 God's Purpose for You is *Salvation.*

What was God's motivation in sending Jesus Christ to earth?

To express His love for you by saving you!

The Bible says, *"God so loved the world that he gave his one and only Son, that whoever believes in him shall not perish but have eternal life. For God did not send his Son into the world to condemn the world, but to save the world through him"* (John 3:16–17).

To forgive your sins, to empower you to have victory over sin, and to enable you to live a fulfilled life!

Jesus said, *"I have come that they may have life, and that they may have it more abundantly"* (John 10:10 NKJV).

#2 Your Problem is *Sin*.

Sin is living independently of God's standard—knowing what is right, but choosing what is wrong.

The Bible says, *"If anyone, then, knows the good they ought to do and doesn't do it, it is sin for them"* (James 4:17).

Spiritual death, eternal separation from God.

Scripture states, *"Your iniquities* [sins] *have separated you from your God"* (Isaiah 59:2).

"The wages of sin is death, but the gift of God is eternal life in Christ Jesus our Lord" (Romans 6:23).

#3 God's Provision for You is the *Savior*.

Yes! Jesus died on the cross to personally pay the penalty for your sins.

The Bible says, *"God demonstrates his own love for us in this: While we were still sinners, Christ died for us"* (Romans 5:8).

What is the solution to being separated from God?

Belief in (entrusting your life to) Jesus Christ as the only way to God the Father.

Jesus says, *"I am the way and the truth and the life. No one comes to the Father except through me"* (John 14:6).

"Believe in the Lord Jesus, and you will be saved" (Acts 16:31).

#4 Your Part is *Surrender.*

Give Christ control of your life, entrusting yourself to Him.

"Jesus said to his disciples, 'Whoever wants to be my disciple must deny themselves and take up their cross [die to your own self-rule] *and follow me. For whoever wants to save their life will lose it, but whoever loses their life for me will find it. What good will it be for someone to gain the whole world, yet forfeit their soul?'"* (Matthew 16:24–26).

Place your faith in (rely on) Jesus Christ as your personal Lord and Savior and reject your "good works" as a means of earning God's approval.

"It is by grace you have been saved, through faith— and this is not from yourselves, it is the gift of God—not by works, so that no one can boast" (Ephesians 2:8–9).

The moment you choose to receive Jesus as your Lord and Savior—entrusting your life to Him—He comes to live inside you. Then He gives you His power to live the fulfilled life God has planned for you. If you want to be fully forgiven by God and become the person God created you to be, you can tell Him in a simple, heartfelt prayer like this:

PRAYER OF SALVATION

"God, I want a real relationship with You.
I admit that many times I've chosen to go
my own way instead of Your way.
Please forgive me for my sins.
Jesus, thank You for dying on the cross to
pay the penalty for my sins.
Come into my life to be my Lord
and my Savior.
Change me from the inside out
and make me the person
You created me to be.
In Your holy name I pray. Amen."

WHAT CAN YOU NOW EXPECT?

If you sincerely prayed this prayer, look at what God says!

> "I will forgive their wickedness and will remember their sins no more."
> (Jeremiah 31:34)

STEPS TO SOLUTION

They're on the prowl! With smooth stealth, they circle quietly, looking intently for the right time to close in on the unguarded. Crouching down, they watch to discover the ones most vulnerable, to detect which sheep are defenseless. Thus, they lie in wait for the weak. Then, to satisfy their insatiable hunger, they slowly move in on the unsuspecting sheep with the most meat, the ones with the most to offer.

When the time is right, they quickly pounce on the unprotected, preying on the powerless. These are "the wolves in sheep's clothing"—the wolves with their woolly masks who mingle among the woolly sheep. These are the ravenous wolves Jesus referred to when He said ...

> "Watch out for false prophets.
> They come to you in sheep's clothing,
> but inwardly they are ferocious wolves."
> (Matthew 7:15)

Open your heart to God, and He will guide you to right living—not through rigid commands or use of power, but through the permanent indwelling of the Holy Spirit. As a Christian, you are completely accepted as His child! Live in the liberty of His love and trust Him to work in you and to change you into the person He created you to be.

Key Passage to Read

LIVE BY FAITH NOT BY THE LAW

"Who has bewitched you?" exclaims the apostle
Paul. He is alarmed that his fellow Christians are
being enticed by false teachers. These legalistic
"law keepers" insist that the young believers must
submit to the old laws because they are *necessary*
for salvation and *necessary* for staying in right
standing in the church.

Upon hearing this, Paul feels passionately
compelled to reemphasize the fact that the
gospel of salvation comes through *faith alone*. He
emphatically refutes the teaching that any legal
requirements are necessary to merit the salvation
of God and reaffirms that we receive the Spirit of
God *only through faith* in the Lord Jesus Christ.
Paul's urgings are for us also.

GALATIANS 3:1–14 (A PARAPHRASE)

▶ Don't be foolish! Don't be duped into believing
that keeping the law will save you. (v. 1)

- ▶ Ask yourself whether you received the Holy Spirit by keeping the law or by placing faith in the message you heard about the gospel. (v. 2)

- ▶ Don't be short-sighted! After beginning your life relying in faith on the Spirit's ability, don't think that you gain success by relying on your human ability to keep the law. (v. 3)

- ▶ Have all your painful experiences under the law been for nothing? (v. 4)

- ▶ Stop and think! Is God working in your life because you have obeyed the law or because you have placed your faith in Jesus Christ? (v. 5)

- ▶ Think about Abraham—God declared him righteous because of his faith. (v. 6)

- ▶ Therefore, all who live by faith are the true children of Abraham. (v. 7)

- ▶ The Scriptures prophesied how even the Gentiles (like Abraham) would be saved through their faith as God had announced to Abraham, *"All nations will be blessed through you."* (v. 8)

- ▶ Therefore, those who have faith are blessed, along with Abraham,who is called *"the man of faith."* (v. 9)

- ▶ If you rely on keeping the law, you are doomed because keeping the law is impossible! (v. 10)

- ▶ No one is saved in God's sight by keeping the law. *"The righteous will live by faith."* (v. 11)

- ▶ The law is not a matter of faith, but a measuring stick of "doing." (v. 12)

▶ Christ has saved us from *"the curse of the law"* by becoming the curse Himself. (v. 13)

▶ God's purpose is plain. The blessing given to Abraham can also reach the Gentiles through Jesus Christ, but it comes only by faith—faith alone! (v. 14)

HOW TO Know the Difference between True Sins & Man-Made Sins

One of the problems Jesus had with the Pharisees was that they added to God's laws by making up laws of their own and then making them equal to God's laws. The result was that the people were burdened down with literally thousands of nitpicky things to remember to do or not to do in order to be right with God.

They were so busy thinking about their actions that they had no time to think about their God or to grow in a personal, intimate relationship with Him; no time to focus on His love, His grace, His mercy, His glory, His character, His goodness, His provision, His compassion, His blessings, His specific plan and purpose for them.

They were unable to distinguish between what man considered a sin and what God considered a sin. That is why Jesus' Sermon on the Mount was revolutionary for them. It opened up the heart of God to them so they might see the spirit of the law in order that they might interpret the law. We have that same need today.

Jesus said ...

*"I tell you that unless your righteousness
surpasses that of the Pharisees
and the teachers of the law, you will
certainly not enter the kingdom of heaven.
You have heard that it was said to the
people long ago ... But I tell you ...
You have heard that it was said ...
But I tell you ... Again, you have heard ...
But I tell you ... You have heard that it was
said ... But I tell you ... You have heard that it
was said ... But I tell you ... "*
*(Matthew 5:20–22, 27–28, 33–34,
38–39, 43–44)*

As you seek to look into the heart of God in order
to distinguish what He considers sin from what
man considers sin, you need to ...

▶ **Ask specific questions.**

- Is it stated as a sin in God's Word?

  *"How can a young person stay on the path
  of purity? By living according to your word"*
  (Psalm 119:9).

- Is it in keeping with following Christ's example?

  *"Do nothing out of selfish ambition or vain
  conceit. Rather, in humility value others above
  yourselves ... have the same mindset as Christ
  Jesus"* (Philippians 2:3, 5).

- Is it glorifying to God?

  "Whether you eat or drink or whatever you do, do it all for the glory of God" (1 Corinthians 10:31).

- Is it a barrier to a Christian brother or sister?

  "Let us stop passing judgment on one another. Instead, make up your mind not to put any stumbling block or obstacle in the way of a brother or sister. I am convinced, being fully persuaded in the Lord Jesus, that nothing is unclean in itself. But if anyone regards something as unclean, then for that person it is unclean. If your brother or sister is distressed because of what you eat, you are no longer acting in love. Do not by your eating destroy someone for whom Christ died. ... It is better not to eat meat or drink wine or to do anything else that will cause your brother or sister to fall" (Romans 14:13–15, 21).

▶ **Be fully convinced in your own mind.**

- If Scripture doesn't clearly address an issue, look for biblical principles that will help you determine whether or not to become involved in that activity.

  "All Scripture is God-breathed and is useful for teaching, rebuking, correcting and training in righteousness, so that the servant of God may be thoroughly equipped for every good work" (2 Timothy 3:16–17).

- Bring questionable areas before the Lord in prayer, asking Him to give you personal convictions about those activities.

  "'I have the right to do anything,' [a popular saying] *you say—but not everything is beneficial.* [Paul is saying] *'I have the right to do anything'—but I will not be mastered by anything"* (1 Corinthians 6:12).

- Realize, the Lord may convict you about something that He doesn't convict someone else about, or vice versa.

  "Each of us will give an account of ourselves to God" (Romans 14:12).

- Don't condemn someone for choosing not to participate with you in something that you think is perfectly acceptable.

  "I am convinced, being fully persuaded in the Lord Jesus, that nothing is unclean in itself. But if anyone regards something as unclean, then for that person it is unclean" (Romans 14:14).

▶ **Use proven principles of decision making.**

- Learn the difference between spiritual commands and social convictions. Make sure you know whether the Bible prohibits a certain action or if that action is just culturally unacceptable to certain people.

  "They worship me in vain; their teachings are merely human rules" (Matthew 15:9).

- Let your own convictions be cultivated. Study the Scriptures and pray that the Lord will show you His heart on certain issues. Write your convictions down on paper and explain why you believe what you believe.

  "Do your best to present yourself to God as one approved, a worker who does not need to be ashamed and who correctly handles the word of truth" (2 Timothy 2:15).

- Limit your liberty out of love. If something is allowable for you but would cause someone else to sin, you are to refrain from that activity. If your behavior merely offends someone but would not cause the person to sin, you are not dealing with a weaker brother but possibly with a legalist.

  "Let us stop passing judgment on one another. Instead, make up your mind not to put any stumbling block or obstacle in the way of a brother or sister" (Romans 14:13).

- Let the Holy Spirit do His job. Allow the Lord to establish His convictions in your heart. But don't try to be someone else's conscience; let the Convictor convict and the Counselor counsel.

  "When he comes, he will prove the world to be in the wrong about sin and righteousness and judgment" (John 16:8).

QUESTION: "What recourse does a son or daughter have with a spiritually abusive parent? How can a parent be confronted and honored at the same time?"

ANSWER: Our heavenly Father is surely greatly saddened when an earthly father misuses His Word to hurt the heart and shatter the soul of one of His children. It is a blow to the very heart of God and a misrepresentation of His character. But how precious to God is the heart of a child—adult or minor—desiring to right a parental wrong in a loving and God-honoring way.

The key to honoring someone is dealing with that person in truth without a hint of hypocrisy. Jesus confronted the spiritual "fathers" of Israel by challenging them with truth. You dishonor someone by withholding a needed confrontation that God could use to bring conviction and change. One approach an adult child might take with an abusive parent could be to say ...

▶ "I want you to know I love you and I want to always act in a way that pleases God and honors you. Therefore, I cannot in good conscience allow you to continue speaking to me in a way that is displeasing to God and puts you in a position of incurring His discipline. God's Word commands us to both encourage and speak kindly to one another and to refrain from association with someone who is easily angered."

▶ "Out of honor to both you and God, I must temporarily leave your presence when you speak to me in a way that violates God's will for me and for you."

▶ "I want to have a wonderful, God-honoring relationship with you, so I pray that you will choose to honor Him by speaking to me in a way that pleases Him and encourages me."

▶ "In the future, I will take any disrespectful language directed toward me to mean that you do not wish to remain in my presence, and I will then leave until another time when we can enjoy each other's company."

A child who lives at home and is dependent on an abusive parent might say something like this ...

▶ "I love you and I believe you love me, but it really hurts me when you say ugly things to me."

▶ "Please ask God to help you not get so angry with me and when you are angry, to be nicer to me."

Since a child cannot easily walk away from a parent, the following "self-talk" might be helpful to ward off the fiery arrows of harsh, harmful speech.

▶ "Dad is not thinking correctly right now and his words are not true."

▶ "God loves me and wants me to believe what He says about me."

▶ "Lord, I ask you to protect my heart from these hurtful words."

▶ "Jesus loves me and gave His life for me."

▶ "The Holy Spirit lives within me and He will help me."

▶ "God, please forgive my daddy, convict him of his sin, and help him to be more like You."

As the apostle Paul instructed the church at Thessalonica, his words are for us as well.

"Take special note of anyone who does not obey our instruction in this letter. Do not associate with them, in order that they may feel ashamed" (2 Thessalonians 3:14).

HOW TO Apply Guidelines in Spiritually Abusive Situations

"Blind guides and hypocrites ... snakes and sons of hell"! That's what Jesus called them.

He could see past the pretension and the pomposity of the Pharisees, stating plainly, *"Everything they do is done for people to see"* (Matthew 23:5). Their long tassels, their priestly robes, their seats of honor in the synagogue didn't impress Jesus—all sickened Him. His warning to us: What may seem sacred might really be sacrilege to God.

"How will you escape being condemned to hell?" (Matthew 23:33). Jesus decries the religious leaders with a litany of rebukes in Matthew chapter 23 for their greed, self-indulgence, legalism, and murderous inclinations against those who are *truly* of God. Seven *"Woe to you"* pronouncements are

made against the Pharisees, who *"do not practice what they preach"* (Matthew 23:3).

Pulpits today are filled with "spiritual" leaders just like the Pharisees who one day will face the same chilling condemnation from Jesus Himself. Therefore, what can you do if you continually find yourself in a spiritually abusive situation?

▶ **Submit** yourself to God's authority. You are accountable to God first and to human authorities second.

"Am I now trying to win the approval of human beings, or of God? Or am I trying to please people? If I were still trying to please people, I would not be a servant of Christ" (Galatians 1:10).

▶ **Talk** about your concerns with spiritual leaders who are not involved in your abusive situation. God desires peace, unity, and reconciliation among Christians.

"Be completely humble and gentle; be patient, bearing with one another in love. Make every effort to keep the unity of the Spirit through the bond of peace" (Ephesians 4:2–3).

▶ **Consider** how the spiritually abusive attitude of others is impacting your spiritual life, your relationships with family members and friends, and your sense of personal value.

"I urge you, brothers and sisters, to watch out for those who cause divisions and put obstacles in your way that are contrary to the teaching you have learned. Keep away from them" (Romans 16:17).

▶ **Separate** yourself from abusive situations and seek out people who are encouraging.

"Encourage one another and build each other up, just as in fact you are doing" (1 Thessalonians 5:11).

QUESTION: "Do I always have to submit to spiritual leaders, even when I know they are abusive? After all, the Bible says, 'Submit yourselves for the Lord's sake to every human authority' (1 Peter 2:13)."

ANSWER: Spiritual abusers love to manipulate others by telling them that they must always submit to spiritual authority. This is wrong! When the apostle Paul was facing trial at the hands of the Jewish religious leaders, he knew he would be executed. Therefore, rather than submitting to religious leaders in Jerusalem who were not following God, Paul appealed to stand trial in Rome before the secular court of Caesar! However, before appealing to Caesar, Paul unknowingly insulted the high priest. When he was told whom he had insulted, Paul agreed that no one should speak evil about the ruler of the Jewish people. Spiritual authority is to be respected always, but obeyed only when it lines up with God's truth.

"At this the high priest Ananias ordered those standing near Paul to strike him on the mouth. Then Paul said to him, 'God will strike you, you whitewashed wall! You sit there to judge me according to the law, yet you yourself violate the law by commanding that I be struck!' Those who

were standing near Paul said, 'How dare you insult God's high priest!' Paul replied, 'Brothers, I did not realize that he was the high priest; for it is written: "Do not speak evil about the ruler of your people"' (Acts 23:2–5).

HOW TO Move from Legalism to Grace

"Amazing grace, how sweet the sound." Who hasn't heard these familiar words that begin what is probably one of the most favored hymns of all time? The author, John Newton (1725–1807), was captain of a ship engaged in slave trade. He transported his share of the 6 million African slaves brought to the Americas during the 18th century. While on a homeward voyage, his ship encountered a violent storm and, fearing all was lost, he exclaimed, "Lord, have mercy on us."

After leaving the slave trade and for the rest of his life, he referred to that day as the day when he understood the *limitless grace of God*. Newton spent the last 43 years of his life as a minister who fully understood the dynamics of *divine grace*— God's gift to everyone irrespective of "good deeds or earned worth." "Amazing Grace" is the means by which we are saved from original sin, given the power to live a life pleasing to God, and granted eternal salvation.

"This righteousness is given through faith in Jesus Christ to all who believe. There is no difference between Jew and

Gentile, for all have sinned
and fall short of the glory of God,
and all are justified freely by his grace
through the redemption that came
by Christ Jesus." (Romans 3:22–24)

"Amazing grace!
How sweet the sound—
That saved a wretch like me!
I once was lost but now am found,
Was blind but now I see.
Through many dangers, toils and snares
I have already come;
'Tis grace hath brought me safe thus far,
And grace will lead me home."[22]

If your heart's desire is to move from legalism to
GRACE, you need to ...

G–GIVE up trying to please God through your
own efforts.

- Understand that the law is not a spiritual code
  for you to follow in order to earn God's favor.

- Understand that you will fail if you think you
  can fulfill the law in your own strength.

- Understand that you need not fear when you
  fail to measure up (and you will). Just rely on
  Christ to be your Redeemer.

Remember, *"There is now no condemnation for
those who are in Christ Jesus, because through*

*Christ Jesus the law of the Spirit who gives life
has set you free from the law of sin and death"*
(Romans 8:1–2).

R**–REALIZE** that God's love is a free gift, complete
and unconditional.

- You are under the "grace principle" of life if
  you are a Christian.

- You have not been delivered from bondage
  in order to focus on a code of rules and
  regulations.

- You need to know that because of the
  everlasting love of the Lord, you are free in
  Christ.

Remember, *"We have been released from the law
so that we serve in the new way of the Spirit, and
not in the old way of the written code"* (Rom. 7:6).

A**–ACCEPT** that Christ through His Holy Spirit is
living in you to empower you to please God.

- Remember, Satan and death and sin were
  defeated at the cross.

- Remember, you received the gifts of salvation,
  eternal life, justification, righteousness, and
  glorification not by any of your own efforts,
  but through faith in Jesus Christ.

- Remember, you died to your old life—and your
  new life is now lived by faith in Christ, who
  earned these things *for* you.

Remember, *"I have been crucified with Christ
and I no longer live, but Christ lives in me. The*

life I now live in the body, I live by faith in the Son of God, who loved me and gave himself for me" (Galatians 2:20).

C–**COMMIT** to reading God's Word.[23]

- Know that the ways of the world are not God's ways.

- Know that by reading the Word of God you will know the ways of God—especially in the areas of your weakness.

- Know that God will use His Word to conform you to His character.

Remember, *"Do not conform to the pattern of this world, but be transformed by the renewing of your mind. Then you will be able to test and approve what God's will is—his good, pleasing and perfect will"* (Romans 12:2).

E–**EXPERIENCE** the freedom of trusting God to fulfill His plan and purpose for you.[24]

- It's up to you to focus on the truth that God promises to complete His purpose for you.

- It's up to you to drop the mentality that "God loves me only when I'm good and rejects me when I'm bad."

- It's up to you to appropriate God's free gift of grace.

Remember, *"Being confident of this, that he who began a good work in you will carry it on to completion until the day of Christ Jesus"* (Philippians 1:6).

Their priorities and practices couldn't have been more different, making one thing perfectly clear: Jesus was indeed the good shepherd—the Pharisees were the false shepherds.

Jesus taught truth.

  Pharisees spread lies.

Jesus embraced sinners.

  Pharisees shunned sinners.

Jesus healed the sick.

  Pharisees hindered the sick.

In the end, the Pharisees fleeced the sheep, whereas Jesus died for the sheep. And Jesus lives today to be *your* shepherd—to shepherd you through life. As you come under His care, putting your total trust in Him, He will be the shepherd of your soul.

> "I am the good shepherd. The good shepherd lays down his life for the sheep."
> (John 10:11)

The following is an acrostic for the word RECOVERY.

R–REALIZE that you have been in a legalistic or abusive situation.

▶ Acknowledge to yourself, to God, and to someone else that you have been spiritually deceived and deeply wounded.

▶ Acknowledge your own willingness to believe the lies you have embraced.

▶ Acknowledge your personal responsibility for propagating those lies to others without personally verifying their validity.

Remember, the Bible says, *"If we confess our sins, he is faithful and just and will forgive us our sins and purify us from all unrighteousness. If we claim we have not sinned, we make him out to be a liar and his word is not in us"* (1 John 1:9–10).

E–**EXERCISE** your freedom in Christ.

▶ Renounce being in bondage to the lies of legalism and embrace the truth that you have been forgiven and set free.

▶ Renounce your excessive allegiance to any spiritual leader or church and embrace Jesus as your spiritual head and leader.

▶ Renounce the laws you have been living under and embrace the One who has set you free from the law.

Remember, the Bible says, *"If the Son sets you free, you will be free indeed"* (John 8:36).

C–**CORRECT** your concept of God.

▶ Study the Bible for yourself to learn the true character of God.

▶ Study the books of Galatians and Hebrews and Romans chapters 3–8, which proclaim your liberty in Christ.

▶ Study the Gospel of John and the Epistle of 1 John to see the loving heart of the Father.

Remember, the Bible says, *"See what great love the Father has lavished on us, that we should be called children of God! And that is what we are! The reason the world does not know us is that it did not know him"* (1 John 3:1).

O–**OPEN** yourself to healthy Christian relationships.

▶ Realize that your fear and distrust of authentic Christians is based on your abusive situation. Then refuse to judge others for the sins of some.

▶ Realize that God created you to be in fellowship with others and that He will use other Christians to bring love, nurturing, and healing to your heart.

▶ Realize that God wants to use you to bring comfort into the lives of others who have also experienced spiritual abuse.

Remember, the Bible says, *"Praise be to the God and Father of our Lord Jesus Christ, the Father of compassion and the God of all comfort, who comforts us in all our troubles, so that we can comfort those in any trouble with the comfort we ourselves receive from God. For just as we share abundantly in the sufferings of Christ, so also our comfort abounds through Christ"* (2 Corinthians 1:3–5).

V–**VOICE** your cares and concerns to God.

▶ Tell God your deepest doubts, hurts, and fears, as well as the deepest longings of your heart.

▶ Tell the Lord about the guilt and anger you feel at being deceived.

▶ Tell the Lord how you feel about being used to satisfy another person's unquenchable hunger for power and position.

Remember, the Bible says, *"Trust in him at all times, you people; pour out your hearts to him, for God is our refuge"* (Psalm 62:8).

E–**ENLIST** the help of spiritually mature, grace-filled mentors.

▶ Seek relationships with those who have unquestioned wisdom and integrity.

▶ Seek those who love the Lord and who cling to the Word as their guide to knowing God.

▶ Seek a spiritual mentor who will encourage you to accurately interpret the Bible for yourself.

Remember, the Bible says, *"Walk with the wise and become wise, for a companion of fools suffers harm"* (Proverbs 13:20).

R–**REST** in the finished work of Christ.

▶ Deny your fleshly compulsion to do "works" in order to gain the approval of God. Claim the righteousness of Christ as your own.

▶ Deny condemning thoughts that assault your mind and your emotions. Claim the cleansing forgiveness of Christ, who has washed you whiter than snow.

▶ Deny the lie that you need to prove yourself worthy of salvation. Claim the fact that God loved you and Jesus died for you in spite of your sin.

Remember, the Bible says, *"At just the right time, when we were still powerless, Christ died for the ungodly. ... But God demonstrates his own love for us in this: While we were still sinners, Christ died for us"* (Romans 5:6, 8).

YIELD yourself to the Holy Spirit, who lives within you.

▶ Trust the Holy Spirit to guide you into truth and to protect you from error.

▶ Trust the Holy Spirit to empower you to love the Lord your God with all your heart, soul, mind, and strength and to live a life that is pleasing to Him and that glorifies Him.

▶ Trust the Holy Spirit to fulfill the promise of God to conform you to the character of Christ.

Remember, the Bible says, *"When he, the Spirit of truth, comes, he will guide you into all truth. He will not speak on his own; he will speak only what he hears, and he will tell you what is yet to come"* (John 16:13).

No one basks in the bountiful riches of God's grace more than the apostle Paul. He is used by God powerfully, yet during his early life he did not know that—apart from the grace of God—he was *a wretched man* (Romans 7:24).

Paul serves God and he struggles with "self," experiencing the spirit and the flesh continually engaged in battle. *"I do not understand what I do. For what I want to do I do not do, but what I hate I do. ... For I have the desire to do what is good, but I cannot carry it out"* (Romans 7:15, 18).

And yet Paul knows he has been saved from ultimate defeat, that his sins are no longer held against him, that separation from a holy God for eternity is not warranted. *Jesus* is his Savior. Therefore, he can stand strong, secure in the riches of God's grace. And so can you because ...

> **"There is now no condemnation for those who are in Christ Jesus."**
> **(Romans 8:1)**

Thank God for His ...

▶ **Saving Grace**

"I know I cannot be saved by keeping the law because the Bible says, *'It is by grace you have been saved, through faith—and this is not from yourselves, it is the gift of God—not by works, so that no one can boast'* (Ephesians 2:8–9)."

"Lord, thank You for the gift of salvation—a gift I do not deserve."

▶ Sustaining Grace

"I know I cannot lose my salvation because the Bible says, *'You also were included in Christ when you heard the message of truth, the gospel of your salvation. When you believed, you were marked in him with a seal, the promised Holy Spirit, who is a deposit guaranteeing our inheritance until the redemption of those who are God's possession—to the praise of his glory'* (Ephesians 1:13–14)."

"Lord, thank You for giving me the gift of eternal life that is guaranteed."

▶ Sufficient Grace

"I know that through my weaknesses, God's power will be perfect within me because the Bible says, *'He* [Jesus] *said to me, "My grace is sufficient for you, for my power is made perfect in weakness." Therefore I* [Paul] *will boast all the more gladly about my weaknesses, so that Christ's power may rest on me'* (2 Corinthians 12:9)."

"Lord, thank You for the gift of Your power—all that I need when experiencing difficulty."

▶ Sanctifying Grace

"I know I have been given victory over sin because the Bible says, *'Sin shall no longer be your master, because you are not under law, but under grace'* (Romans 6:14)."

"Lord, thank You for the gift of Your grace to live a godly life."

▶ Satisfying Grace

"I know that because of God's mercy, I can experience complete satisfaction because the Bible says, *'Praise be to the God and Father of our Lord Jesus Christ! In his great mercy he has given us new birth into a living hope through the resurrection of Jesus Christ from the dead, and into an inheritance that can never perish, spoil or fade. This inheritance is kept in heaven for you'* (1 Peter 1:3–4)."

"Lord, thank You for giving me the gifts of a living hope and an inheritance that can never perish, spoil, or fade."

In the essentials, unity.
In the nonessentials, liberty.
And in all things, charity.

Precious child of God, you don't need
to work or to do one more act
to gain God's approval.
You have His approval—
you are accepted by the Beloved!

—June Hunt

SCRIPTURES TO MEMORIZE

Why does God make salvation a **gift through faith** and **not by works**?

*"It is by grace you have been saved, **through faith** —and this is not from yourselves, it is the **gift** of God—**not by works**, so that no one can boast."* (Ephesians 2:8–9)

If we have been **made right with God through faith**, do we still **need the law**?

*"The law was our guardian until Christ came; it protected us until we could be **made right with God through faith**. And now that the way of faith has come, we no longer **need the law** as our guardian."* (Galatians 3:24–25 NLT)

Since I can't become **righteous by** my **works**, what is the purpose of **the law**?

*"No one will be declared **righteous** in God's sight **by** the **works** of the law; rather, through **the law** we become conscious of our sin."* (Romans 3:20)

From what has **Christ set us free**?

*"It is for freedom that **Christ** has **set us free**. Stand firm, then, and do not let yourselves be burdened again by a yoke of slavery."* (Galatians 5:1)

If righteousness could be gained through the law, what would that say about **Christ**?

*"I do not set aside the grace of God, for **if righteousness could be gained through the law, Christ** died for nothing!"* (Galatians 2:21)

Is my spirituality **judged** by what I **eat or drink** or whether I keep the **Sabbath day**?

*"Do not let anyone **judge** you by what you **eat or drink**, or with regard to a religious festival, a New Moon celebration or a **Sabbath day**. These are a shadow of the things that were to come; the reality, however, is found in Christ."* (Colossians 2:16–17)

What does the Bible say about **trying to please people** and not being able to say *no*?

*"Am I now trying to win the approval of human beings, or of God? Or am I trying to please people? If I were still **trying to please people**, I would not be a servant of Christ."* (Galatians 1:10)

Is Saturday a day that is **more sacred than another day**?

*"One person considers one **day more sacred than another**; another considers every day alike. Each of them should be fully convinced in their own mind."* (Romans 14:5)

Why should **sin no longer be** my **master**?

*"**Sin** shall **no longer be** your **master**, because you are not under the law, but under grace."* (Romans 6:14)

After the passing of the Old Testament Law, is there no **covenant** to live by? Are there no **laws**?

*"This is the **covenant** I will make with them after that time, says the Lord. I will put my **laws** in their hearts, and I will write them on their minds."* (Hebrews 10:16)

NOTES

1. Edward J. Cumella, "Religious Abuse," *The Remuda Review*, spring 2005, vol. 4, issue 2, 17.

2. David Johnson and Jeff VanVonderen, *The Subtle Power of Spiritual Abuse: Recognizing and Escaping Spiritual Manipulation and False Spiritual Authority Within the Church* (Minneapolis, MN: Bethany House, 1991), 20.

3. Ken Blue, *Healing Spiritual Abuse: How to Break Free from Bad Church Experiences* (Downers Grove: InterVarsity Press, 1993), 44–48; Johnson and Van Vonderen, *The Subtle Power of Spiritual Abuse,* 37–39.

4. *Merriam-Webster's Collegiate Dictionary,* electronic edition (NY: Merriam-Webster, 2001), s.v. "Legal."

5. Charles C. Ryrie, *Balancing the Christian Life: Biblical Principles for Wholesome Living* (Chicago: Moody, 1969), 159.

6. C. I. Scofield, *Rightly Dividing the Word of Truth: Ten Outline Studies of the More Important Divisions of Scripture* (Neptune, NJ: Loizeaux Brothers, 1896), 44–45.

7. W. E. Vine, Merrill F. Unger, and William White, *Vine's Complete Expository Dictionary of Biblical Words*, electronic ed. (Nashville: Thomas Nelson, 1996).

8. Bob George, Discipleship Counseling Services, *Discipleship Counseling Training Student Manual* (Dallas: Discipleship Counseling Services, n.d.).

9. Cumella, "Religious Abuse," 17–18.

10. David A. Seamands, *Healing Grace* (Wheaton, IL: Victor, 1988), 18–19.

11. Seamands, *Healing Grace*, 100–106.

12. Cumella, "Religious Abuse," 18.

13. Cumella, "Religious Abuse," 18.

14. Cumella, "Religious Abuse," 18.

15. Seamands, *Healing Grace*, 126–138.

16. Cumella, "Religious Abuse," 18.

17. Seamands, *Healing Grace*, 12–14.

18. Cumella, "Religious Abuse," 19; Seamands, *Healing Grace*, 19.

19. Seamands, *Healing Grace* (Wheaton, IL: Victor, 1988), 12–19.

20. Stephen Arterburn and Jack Felton, *Toxic Faith: Understanding and Overcoming Religious Addiction* (Nashville: Thomas Nelson, 1991), 265–314.

21. Lawrence J. Crabb, Jr., *Understanding People: Deep Longings for Relationship*, Ministry Resources Library (Grand Rapids: Zondervan, 1987), 15–16; Robert S. McGee, *The Search for Significance*, 2nd ed. (Houston, TX: Rapha, 1990), 27–30.

22. John Newton, "Amazing Grace" in *Olney Hymns* (London: W. Oliver, 1779).

23. David R. Miller, *Breaking Free: Rescuing Famlies from the Clutches of Legalism* (Grand Rapids: Baker, 1992), 174–175.

24. Kevin A. Miller, "I Don't Feel Like a Very Good Christian: Why Does It Seem That You Can Never Quite Measure Up?", *Discipleship Journal*, September/October 1988, 9.

HOPE FOR THE HEART TITLES

www.aspirepress.com